D1541152

AUSTRALIA'S SCENIC COASTLINE

From the Great Ocean Road, Victoria

AUSTRALIA'S SCENIC COASTLINE

Jocelyn Burt

RIGBY

Acknowledgments

I am indebted to many people for their help in the preparation of this book. In particular I would like to thank Evelyn Richards of the Orchid Beach Island Resort, Fraser Island; Fitz McLean of the Brampton Island Resort; John Dyke of The Lodge, Rottnest Island; Allen Mulder of Wild Country Safaris, Mackay; Ray Coster of Dunk Island; and Dieter Voitl of Malua Bay.

National Library of Australia
Cataloguing-in-publication entry

Burt, Jocelyn.
    Australia's scenic coastline.
    ISBN 0 7270 0914 1
    1. Coasts—Australia—Pictorial works. I. Title.

919.4'00222

RIGBY LIMITED ● ADELAIDE ● SYDNEY
MELBOURNE ● BRISBANE ● PERTH
First published 1978
Copyright © Jocelyn Burt, 1978
All rights reserved
Wholly designed and set up in Australia
Printed in Hong Kong

Introduction

Australia is the world's smallest continent, but its 38 000-kilometre coastline provides as great a diversity of scenic beauty and character as the land it borders. Coastal plains and mountains end abruptly at rock-encrusted shores or sheer off into spectacular, sometimes terrifyingly steep cliffs. Remarkable landforms occur in many places, some boldly prominent, there for the world to see; others concealing their weird or spectacular formations in rugged terrain. Magnificent beaches curve into the coast between craggy headlands washed by turbulent surf or stretch, unbroken, for vast golden distances. Inlets and lagoons offer tranquillity, and estuaries, sand-barred or widely flowing, gently punctuate the seaboard. Scores of islands lie offshore, many of them very beautiful and touched with more than a hint of romance.

Seven seas surround this land, continually shaping it by the action of their waves. As is to be expected in a country that has its northern regions lying in tropical seas and its southern coastline in the cold waters of a temperate zone, there are enormous climatic variations, and these affect the shores in many different ways. No land mass lies between the Antarctic and Australia, and as a result the south coast is frequently exposed to storms born in the tempestuous Southern Ocean. The great rollers of the Indian Ocean wash the shores of Western Australia, but in the north-west of the continent, the Great Barrier Reef protects the coast to a large degree from the rough seas of the Pacific. The shores of the north lie in peace during the Dry season, but during the Wet they are lashed by monsoonal rains and cyclonic winds that can cause untold damage.

Australians love the coastline of their country, and enjoy the myriad attractions it has to offer. Its many contrasting faces and ever-changing moods evoke different responses in those who visit it; but, once caught in the spell of that magic combination of sea and shore, the visitor is drawn back time and time again.

Facing page:
The Twelve Apostles, Port Campbell, Victoria

Below:
The Hazards, Tasmania

Cliffs, Rocks and Coastal Mountains

The sight of a line of vertical cliffs plunging many metres to the ocean below can be both awe-inspiring and humbling: seldom does man feel less significant than when faced with the enormity and power of a dramatic seascape. There is fear, too, and reluctance to venture too close to the cliff edge, but the attraction of the promised spectacle is mesmeric, and few do not succumb. So we peer fearfully into the dizzying depths below, watching in admiration as the distant swell heaves and pounds against the bare cliff face. The hollow booming of the water as it surges into hidden caves and crevasses magnifies the atmosphere of eeriness and supernatural power.

A large portion of Australia's shoreline is bound by cliffs and rocky belts, and this is where some of the continent's most dramatic coastal scenery is found. If access is easy, these areas are always well visited, regardless of the weather—especially during holiday times. One of the most popular areas for sightseeing is the region that lies within the Port Campbell National Park, on the south-west coast of Victoria. Here a spectacular line of cliffs runs for many kilometres from Peterborough to near Princeton. Some of the vertically-walled headlands have been fashioned into natural bridges and archways by wave erosion, and towering residual stacks rise out of the sea in majestic splendour. The most famous of these is the group known as the Twelve Apostles. It is easy to view these astonishing natural phenomena, for the road runs close to the coast, and several lookouts have been established in the area.

Another extraordinary region that has in recent times been made accessible to the public is that part of the Great Australian Bight which is bordered by a huge wall of cliffs. At the numerous viewing points set beside the Nullarbor's Eyre Highway, there is no shortage of notices warning of the very real dangers that threaten the over-intrepid. All along this great line of cliffs there are alarming overhanging sections, some of which give the uncomfortable feeling that it would take only a few heavy footsteps to make the fragile-looking edges break away altogether.

Undoubtedly the cliffs that border the Bight are the most awe-inspiring, but many others hold a similar fascination—especially those on the east coast of Tasmania's Tasman Peninsula, in the areas just north and south of Sydney, and on the west coast of the Eyre Peninsula. In the latter area, Point Labatt is of considerable interest, because at the base of the magnificent cliffs there is a colony of Sea Lions.

Coastal hills and mountains have a gentler but equally impressive beauty. Where roads have been carved into their steep slopes, as with the Great Ocean Road west of Geelong and the Cook Highway that links Cairns and Port Douglas, the scenery is wonderful. The south coast of New South Wales also has spectacular areas where the mountains finally give on to the seacoast in a series of rugged cliffs.

Rocks, too, play a large part in giving to each part of Australia's coast its unique identity. Pounded by waves, they are continually eroded and reshaped, changing the whole face of the seaboard. They stud hills and headlands in smooth slabs or craggy boulders, or lie in great jumbled heaps at the water's edge to provide a paradise for children and rockhounds. They stand on windswept beaches as isolated tors, or balance precariously on top of one another, or spread out in rocky platforms like massive aprons. In colour, shape, size, and origin, their diversity is marvellous.

POINT LABATT, SOUTH AUSTRALIA
Shrouded in sea mist, these towering walls of rock line a section of the west coast of Eyre Peninsula, south of Streaky Bay.

Previous pages:
TERRIGAL, NEW SOUTH WALES
Terrigal lies on the northern outskirts of Greater Sydney, ninety-five kilometres from the city, and is one of many towns that cluster along the cliff tops of this region. Much of the coast in the area is characterised by its contrasting scenic attractions. Massive headlands rise from rugged, sometimes treacherous rocky platforms that give way at intervals to wide, sweeping beaches of golden sand washed by the rolling surf of the Pacific Ocean. There are magnificent views from the roads that meander over the coastal hilltops: one of Terrigal's best vantage points is from the cliff by the oval.

Above:
THE BIGHT, SOUTH AUSTRALIA
The magnificent line of sea cliffs that borders the Great Australian Bight is the longest in the world. Stretching for 200 kilometres and in places plunging nearly 100 metres to the ocean below, they are also one of the most awe-inspiring sights of the Australian coastline. The re-making in the 1970s of the Eyre Highway, which crosses the Nullarbor Plain and links the eastern States with the west, has enabled motorists to see the cliffs to their best advantage. There are six different lookout points situated close to the road between Nullarbor and the Western Australian border.

NEAR CAIRNS, QUEENSLAND

The Kuranda road that winds down the slopes of the Atherton Tableland to Cairns provides some wonderful vistas of the surrounding countryside, with mountains falling away to plains chequered with canefields that stretch almost to the boundaries of the city. The same views can be obtained from the train that runs from the picturesque Kuranda railway station to Cairns, and many tourists prefer to make this trip. Situated around mountain-edged Trinity Bay in one of the loveliest natural settings of all Australia's coastal cities, Cairns has become a mecca for southerners escaping cold winters. It is also the home port for the great 'Marlin Meet', held yearly for fishermen from all parts of the globe to try for the next marlin world record. The season extends from September to December, at the time of the Black Marlin migration from the waters around Papua New Guinea into the southbound currents. The giant fish are caught as they cruise along in the deep waters along the ocean side of the Great Barrier Reef. Although some visitors arrive for the Meet in their own yachts, there are launches for hire, equipped for big game fishing and manned by experienced crews. Official weighing stations are provided at Cairns, Lizard Island, Cooktown, and Innisfail.

Left:
TASMAN ARCH, TASMANIA
Over the ages, hungry waves have relentlessly eaten into the rocky shoreline on the eastern side of the Tasman Peninsula, near Eaglehawk Neck, to fashion this spectacular natural bridge. On stormy days the sea crashes through the fifty-three metres high arch and pours into the inlet, giving it the appearance of a massive boiling cauldron. There are many fascinating and well-known coastal sights in this area, including the Devil's Kitchen, caves and blowholes, and the amazing Tessellated Pavement. The Tasman Peninsula is linked to the Forestier Peninsula at Eaglehawk Neck by a thread of land only eighteen metres wide.

Above:
WHALERS WAY, SOUTH AUSTRALIA
Waves borne on a monstrous swell burst against the rocks and explode high into the air at Cape Carnot, thirty-two kilometres from Port Lincoln. Now situated on private property, this section of the coast, known as the Whalers Way, was once the site for considerable whaling activity. The scenic drive runs fifteen kilometres along the southernmost tip of Eyre Peninsula, which offers a wide variety of rugged beauty in its plunging cliffs and rocky bays. To enter this area it is necessary to have a permit and a key, obtainable in the town of Port Lincoln.

THE PAINTED CLIFFS, TASMANIA

During the convict days Maria Island was established as a penitentiary, but today it enjoys a gentler existence as a national park, providing safe breeding grounds for two species threatened with extinction—the Forestier Kangaroo and the Cape Barren Goose. Park rangers have the dual function of protecting the environment and looking after the island's historic buildings. Tourists also come to Maria Island to view its many scenic features. These beautifully coloured cliffs lie at the southern end of Hopground Beach, two kilometres from Darlington along the coast road. Continual weathering by wind and waves has created unusual patterns in the sandstone so that in parts it resembles a honeycomb filled with whorls of chocolate and cream.

STANWELL PARK, NEW SOUTH WALES

The wide open beaches along the coast south of Sydney are interspersed with cliffs and high country which give breathtaking views of the surrounding countryside. This photograph was taken from the Lawrence Hargrave Lookout, which is perched high on a hilltop beside the Princes Highway, sixty-six kilometres from Sydney. Because of the lookout's elevation, it gives an almost aerial panorama of the country below—a fitting memorial to the man whose pioneering research in aeronautics played such a vital part in the development of the aeroplane. Much of Hargrave's work was carried out at Stanwell Park in the early 1890s. Today the area is a paradise for hang-gliding enthusiasts.

17

Above:

JIMMY NEWHILLS HARBOUR, WESTERN AUSTRALIA

South of Albany, on the ocean side of the peninsula that embraces King George Sound, the granite coastline has been formed into many striking inlets, gorges, and chasms. A large proportion of this magnificent scenic area lies in the Torndirrup National Park. At Jimmy Newhills Harbour there is a lookout which gives a dramatic view of the steep slopes that plunge to the very narrow inlet of the harbour itself. Albany lies on the southern seaboard of Western Australia, 410 kilometres from Perth.

Top right:

GANTHEAUME POINT, WESTERN AUSTRALIA

The coast around Broome has many colourful scenic spots, but Gantheaume Point, with its startlingly red rocks giving on to brilliant tropical waters, is one of the most spectacular. The area has an additional attraction in the form of the fossilised footprints of a dinosaur, embedded in rock some thirty metres out to sea. However, these are visible only at extreme low tides.

Bottom right:

PORTSEA, VICTORIA

This dramatically-shaped rock known as the London Bridge lies at one end of the Portsea ocean beach on the Mornington Peninsula, ninety-five kilometres from Melbourne.

18

Left:

KALBARRI, WESTERN AUSTRALIA

This is Red Bluff, which forms part of the coastline of the Kalbarri National Park, north of Geraldton. Situated near the mouth of the Murchison River and intersected by gullies and headlands, the bluff rises high above the sea in tiers and overhanging ledges of layered sandstone. Visitors are fascinated by the strange formations and the enormous variety of textures, colours, and patterns contained within these rocks. So convoluted is the coast here that it is possible to stand at the very edge of a cliff and hear the surf thundering eerily in a cave immediately below your feet.

Above:

WILSONS PROMONTORY

Mount Ramsay, Mount Latrobe, and the Mount Vereker Range provide a magnificent backdrop for the serenity of Sealers Cove on Wilsons Promontory. During the summer months flocks of visiting Crested Terns can often be seen here, winging their way across the water. Access to this lovely spot is by a walking track that starts from the car park on the other side of the range. Hikers generally allow five or six hours to reach the cove. The steep, granite-studded promontory, part of Gippsland, is the most southerly point of the Australian continent.

Dunes and Beaches

Australia is renowned for her wide, sweeping beaches: many say they are among the world's finest. Some of them run on and on, sweeping unbroken to the distant horizon and earning such names as the Seventy-Five Mile Beach, the Eighty Mile Beach, and the Ninety Mile Beach. Many others, less extensive, are still wide and spacious, providing an inviting stretch of sand between vegetation and waterline. Some of these, like Norman Beach at Wilsons Promontory, Broome's Cable Beach, and those beaches north of Sydney, epitomise the essential and precious freedom that is so dear to the hearts of Australians.

There are small beaches, too. Some are pocket-sized, fitting neatly between great bastions of rocks or craggy headlands, or tucked away in coves. These small sanctuaries offer privacy and seclusion for those who wish to escape the hordes of summer holidaymakers that flock to the larger beaches. Some beaches provide ideal venues for swimmers and board-riders, others a quiet haven for fishermen, sailing enthusiasts, or family groups for whom the joys of a seaside holiday include all the time-honoured pursuits of fishing, crabbing, paddling, or looking for shells.

The Australians' love for their beaches is not restricted to the summer months. All year round dedicated walkers and joggers can enjoy a brisk tramp or trot along the water's edge, breathing in the invigorating ozone-filled air. Dune-buggy riding is rapidly growing in popularity—much to the alarm of conservationists—and, regardless of the weather, board-riders dressed in wetsuits can be seen bobbing in the waves like great black waterbirds as they wait to catch a good breaker.

Although there are many good beaches with water safe for bathing, strong and often treacherous surf washes a large part of the coastline. Fortunately, swimming on the ocean beaches has been made much safer by the dedicated work of lifesaving clubs scattered all around Australia in the more densely populated areas.

Most would agree that the type of sand to be found on a beach largely determines its character and attractiveness. Around Australia's coastline its colour varies from pure white, through all the shades of gold and light brown, to red. Much of the sand is fine—indeed, it is so fine in parts of southwest Western Australia that it squeaks underfoot, and when pressed in the hand feels like talcum powder. Sand even finer than this lies in the Cape Arid region, west of the Bight. This can be treacherous, because it acts like dry quicksand, capable of swallowing vehicles and men alike—as some have discovered to their horror.

Many beaches are flanked by dunes which are generally stabilised to varying degrees by vegetation. However, sometimes a 'blowout' or 'sandblow' occurs, when the efficiency of the frail plant cover is so weakened by strong winds that the dunes start to move, covering everything in their path. Causes other than natural ones can wreak the same havoc. Often the overgrazing of animals, or the careless use of heavy vehicles in sandy areas can destroy vegetation that is only just managing to anchor the vast hills of sand. The balance between blowout and stabilisation is a very fine one—often even the slightest disturbance will start the sand moving. Nevertheless, great beauty is often revealed in great wind-moulded expanses of sand like those on Fraser Island or along the shores of the Great Australian Bight.

NAMBUCCA HEADS, NEW SOUTH WALES
There are many good views of splendid beaches from various vantage points set high on the cliff tops of this coastal town north of Sydney.

Previous pages:
PETERBOROUGH, VICTORIA
Australia's beaches, with their wide stretches of
sand, are ideal venues for the surf carnivals that
take place every summer in all States. These
events are always very popular with the public,
who come to see boat drill, parade marching, and
surf races held between local and visiting clubs.
Visitors can also learn something of beach safety
measures and see lifesaving demonstrations. The
surf lifesaving movement, a remarkable
humanitarian service, was born in Australia at the
turn of the century. It enables thousands of people to swim in safety under the watchful eyes of
skilled lifesavers—all of whom work on a volun-
tary basis.

Above:
FOUR MILE BEACH, QUEENSLAND
The best view of this splendid beach that sweeps
along the coast at Port Douglas in northern
Queensland can be obtained from the town's
lookout on Flagstaff Hill. At one time cars and
even tourist coaches were allowed on the beach,
which at low tide provided an astonishingly wide
highway of hard sand, but today it is closed to all
vehicular traffic. The small town lying behind the
beach is rich in historic associations. During the
goldrush days of the 1880s it rivalled Cairns in
size and importance, but with the cessation of
mining it became a quiet little fishing village, full
of character and charm.

EUCLA, WESTERN AUSTRALIA

Some of Australia's most spectacular coastal dunes are these at Eucla, situated near the South Australian border on the lonely shores of the Great Australian Bight. The best times to explore the dunes are at dawn and dusk, when the shadows of the low sun give them an unearthly, sculpted appearance. Except for the area around the ruins of Eucla's historic telegraph station and the path that leads to the beach, the dunes are virtually untouched by human footprints. Originally these great mounds of sand were anchored by vegetation, but by the end of the nineteenth century armies of introduced rabbits had reached Eucla, and in a short time had devoured enough of this plant cover to allow massive wind erosion. Now, driven by strong southerlies, the dunes are constantly on the move, and have all but swallowed the ruins of the old telegraph station. This well-known landmark was built in 1877 to provide a direct link between the eastern States and Western Australia, but in 1920 a new telegraph line was opened along the railway, situated well to the north. The new Eucla settlement has been built on a hilltop beside the Eyre Highway, five kilometres from the dunes.

27

ESPERANCE, WESTERN AUSTRALIA

Many beaches of fine white sand guarded by granite rocks and headlands line the coast around Esperance, while offshore lie the myriad islands of the Archipelago of the Recherche. From the town itself there is a delightful scenic drive along the cliff tops to Twilight Cove—a trip that is a 'must' for visitors. Although some of the beaches are excellent for swimming, others can be very dangerous, and so the local Shire Council has erected warning signs where necessary. There are more superb beaches and a variety of scenic attractions in the Cape Le Grand National Park, fifty-six kilometres away.

28

COOLOOLA SANDS, QUEENSLAND

One of the most popular day trips for tourists in the Noosa Heads district north of Brisbane is a visit to the coloured sands of Teewah Beach. Vivid-hued sandstone bluffs and canyons line the beach for approximately thirty kilometres, rising in places to heights of over sixty metres. These fascinating geological formations are the remains of a system of iron-stained dunes, deposited many thousands of years ago when the sea level was much lower. Although they appear solid in structure, the dunes are really very fragile. Beneath the fine crust the sand will crumble at the lightest touch.

Top left:
NEAR PORTLAND, VICTORIA
The long line of sand-dunes that flanks Discovery Bay starts at the back of Bridgewater, about twenty kilometres from Portland in the far south-western corner of Victoria. A good view of the dunes can be obtained from the lookout beside the Portland-Nelson road.

Bottom left:
LAURIETON, NEW SOUTH WALES
Capped with plumes of flying white spray, large rolling waves from the Pacific wash the beach that lies close to the small town of Laurieton, on the north coast.

Above:
BROOME, WESTERN AUSTRALIA
Cable Beach is situated only a few kilometres away from the town centre of Broome, on the far north-western coast. Its fine, soft sands stretch for twenty-two kilometres, and at times the width of the beach from dunes to waterline is a good 200 metres. The size and spaciousness of the beach are matched by its unusual beauty. The smooth sands are bordered here and there by vibrantly coloured sand-dunes, and rocks splashed with the same bright tints are scattered in profusion near the main swimming area. Gantheaume Point, at the far end of Cable Beach, is also famous for its striking colouration.

MALUA BAY, NEW SOUTH WALES

This small beach is at Garden Bay, one of several delightful coves that notch the shores of Malua Bay, situated just south of Batemans Bay on the south coast. The settlement consists mainly of holiday homes, many of which nestle among the trees on the wooded headlands and command magnificent views of the coast. Skin-diving is popular here, for not only is there good underwater scenery, but the local fishing grounds are rich in prawns, crayfish, abalone, snapper and flathead. Offshore lie the Tollgate Islands, two rocky outcrops which, as nature reserves, provide a haven for some penguins and a multitude of other birds.

PORT WILLUNGA, SOUTH AUSTRALIA

Situated in the region known locally as the South Coast, Port Willunga lies about forty-five kilometres south of Adelaide. It is one of a number of seaside beauty spots, from Port Noarlunga to Sellicks Beach, that have become popular resorts, with small communities of weekend and permanent houses. The beaches in this area are lined by soft, sandy cliffs of warm yellow-brown colours that afford quite a different sort of beauty from that seen in the rest of Australia's coastline. In many places the cliffs are cracked and fissured, and at Port Willunga some of them are topped with clay domes that stand out against the horizon in dramatic relief when the sun is low in the sky.

Estuaries, Inlets and Coastal Lakes

Some of the most tranquil coastal scenes lie where watercourses spill into lagoons sheltering behind barriers of sand, or where rivers empty into inlets and widen out to estuaries before meeting the sea. Australia has many such places along its shores, some of them arrestingly beautiful. At these spots it is not hard to find peace and contentment, especially in the early and late hours of the day.

The soft dawn light can transform the quiet waters of lakes and lagoons into avenues of enchantment, bathing them in subtle shimmering colours that no human artist could hope to match. Sometimes, on chill mornings, their beauty is given an added air of mystery by a cloak of soft white mist that lingers lazily over the still water. With the rising sun, breezes come to lift the vaporous clouds and to ruffle the smooth surface; and when these have died, the water becomes a gigantic mirror, reflecting deeply everything around it—vegetation, sand-dunes, wooded hills, houses, jetties, and moored boats. But usually the perfection of the mirror is brief. Perhaps an intrusion into the scene by living things will actually enhance its beauty, as when a small armada of swans or pelicans sails over the glassy water, or when a flock of cormorants leaves its perching place to indulge in some fishing. But when a screaming speedboat cuts through the mirror, turning it into a series of fluid corrugations, the mood is shattered completely.

It is small wonder that people return year after year to the shores of a quiet lagoon or estuary for their holidays—sometimes even retiring to a permanent life there. One need spend only a day at such havens as Mallacoota in the far south-east corner of Gippsland, or Western Australia's Nornalup Inlet, or Moruya Heads on the south coast of New South Wales, to understand the attraction of these places. Often the settlements at river-mouths and around lagoons originated as bases for fishermen, but today many of the local residents depend more on tourism for their livelihoods than on the fishing industry.

All estuaries, inlets, and coastal lagoons are naturally influenced to some degree by the tides, which affect their water salinity. When the balance is deliberately upset by man's interference, more drastic changes take place—almost invariably to the detriment of the place concerned. This is happening, for example, at Gippsland Lakes, where the salinity has increased substantially since the artificial entrance from the ocean was made in 1890. The vegetation that once bound the silt and sand in swamps and deltas has died, with the result that now the river sediment is settling on the beds of the lakes and gradually filling them up. Another place that has seen vast changes since the days of white settlement is the Coorong, which has been affected by the draining and clearing of land and the erection of the barrages that hold back fresh water just above the mouth of the Murray River.

A few inlets and lagoons lie in national parks, which afford some protection for the flora and fauna usually found in abundance in these areas.

LAKE WEYBA, QUEENSLAND
Lake Weyba, fed by the Noosa River, is linked to several other beautiful lakes that stretch for many kilometres close to the coast before emptying into Laguna Bay.

WALLIS LAKE, NEW SOUTH WALES

Situated on the north coast about 230 kilometres from Sydney, Wallis Lake is the largest in the system of lagoons known as the Great Lakes, all of which are fed by numerous creeks and rivers. The waters of Wallis Lake at its estuary provide excellent conditions for oyster cultivation, and today this is an important industry for the twin towns of Forster and Tuncurry. An Oyster Festival, held each year, attracts many visitors. The colourful sailing regatta staged on Wallis Lake at this time is one of the largest held in New South Wales, and takes place over a course of twenty kilometres.

MALLACOOTA INLET, VICTORIA

One of the loveliest inlets of the Australian coastline is at Mallacoota, which lies in the far eastern corner of Gippsland, 490 kilometres from Melbourne. Here over 4500 hectares of land around the shoreline have been set aside as a national park, for, as well as being scenically very beautiful, the area contains an abundance of native flora and fauna that must be protected. The inlet was formed from the silting up of the Genoa River and the drowning of the river valley. Mallacoota provides amenities for holidaymakers and serves as a base for the fishermen who harvest its abalone beds—the richest in Australia.

BLACKWOOD RIVER, WESTERN AUSTRALIA

The Blackwood River winds for just over 300 kilometres through rich, heavily-timbered rural land in the south-west of Western Australia, receiving the waters of many tributaries before it empties into the sea near Cape Leeuwin. The picturesque river-mouth is the site for the town of Augusta, which in the summer months is a haven for tourists, particularly keen fishermen. Often, in the later afternoon, pelicans gather at various spots along this part of the river, for they know there is a good chance that fishermen cleaning their catch will give them tidbits. The sight of these stately birds scrambling in the water to snatch the thrown morsels is both impressive and comical: for once the greedy seagulls, always alert for a handout, find that the competition is just too fierce. The attractive lighthouse at Cape Leeuwin, not far from the town, stands on the extreme south-west point of the continent, where the Southern and Indian oceans meet. From the hills near Augusta there are some excellent views of the rugged coast and the promontory on which the lighthouse stands.

Above:

MARGARET RIVER, WESTERN AUSTRALIA

A short distance from the Margaret River township, 280 kilometres south of Perth, the river itself enters the sea. In summer the mouth is blocked by a sandbar, with the result that the river waters spread out to form a lake. There are many attractions here. The beach by the river-mouth provides excellent surf for board-riding enthusiasts, and the surrounding countryside, with its undulating, tree-studded hills, is renowned for its extensive system of spectacular caves — well over 200 in all. At present only the Mammoth, Lake, and Jewel caves are open to the public.

Following pages:

MORUYA HEADS, NEW SOUTH WALES

The small holiday settlement of Moruya Heads lies six kilometres from Moruya on the southern seaboard, in the region popularly known as 'the Sapphire coast'. Here the Moruya River opens into a charming inlet set against the splendid backdrop of the Great Dividing Range. As with other estuaries in this section of the coast, oyster farming is extensively carried out in the Moruya River. Some of the best vantage points for views over the area can be obtained from the slopes of the headland that guards the estuary. On the ocean side, surf breaks on the long stretch of golden sand that sweeps around the bay.

39

Above:
LAKES ENTRANCE, VICTORIA
This manmade entrance provides access from the sea to the extensive estuarine system of the Gippsland Lakes that lies behind the Ninety Mile Beach. Before 1890, when the entrance was cut, the lakes were sealed from the ocean by a sandbar. Over the years the incoming seawater has increased the salinity of the lakes, and this in turn has upset the delicate ecology of the system. The town of Lakes Entrance is situated on the eastern side of the artificial inlet. It is both a popular resort and the base for a large fishing fleet: at dawn on most mornings, visitors to the town's lookout can see the boats setting out for a day's fishing.

Top right:
THE COORONG, SOUTH AUSTRALIA
The sun sets over Younghusband Peninsula, the strip of land that separates the waters of the Coorong from the ocean. For 130 kilometres this long, narrow lagoon curves southward from the Murray River mouth, providing a sanctuary for a wide variety of birds.

Bottom right:
ENDEAVOUR RIVER, QUEENSLAND
From Cooktown's Grassy Hill there is a magnificent panorama of the Endeavour River estuary. It was here, in 1770, that Captain Cook repaired his damaged ship *Endeavour* before continuing his voyage up the eastern coast.

Tropical Shores

Much of Australia's northern coastline is washed by tropical seas. The area takes in Broome and the Kimberleys in the far northwest of Australia; all the coastline of the Northern Territory; and a large part of the Queensland coast extending from the Gulf of Carpentaria, taking in all of Cape York Peninsula, and reaching around to Ingham on the eastern seaboard.

Large areas of the tropical coast are still virgin ground. New regions are bound to be developed in the future, but there will be parts that in all probability will remain wilderness because of the difficulty of access either by land or sea. This applies particularly to much of the vast Kimberley region. Its wild and fragmented rocky shores are well guarded on the seaward side by innumerable reefs and unpredictable tides, and from the land by formidably rugged country. There are three major settlements along this part of the coast, all accessible by road: Broome, Derby, and Wyndham. Broome has some strikingly-coloured coastal scenery in its rocks and beaches, but Derby's unique beauty is best seen from the air, as the town is almost surrounded by extensive areas of mudflats and mangroves. Tidal erosion has etched into the soft ground of the mudflats an amazing display of patterns that resemble giant trees and ferns; but unfortunately their extent and intricacy can only be seen from an aircraft. The landscape around Wyndham is different again. Seen from the summit of a nearby hill, the view of Cambridge Gulf and the surrounding countryside reveals in all its uncompromising harshness the character of this merciless land.

Here and there along the coast of the Northern Territory are forests of mangroves. These strange, tangled trees barricade huge tracts of swampland—country so uninviting that even if man could get past the constricting vegetation, he would have little desire to stay. Sometimes the mangrove forests give way to areas of sand edged with other tropical vegetation that has had a chance to become established and survive. Mangroves are very much a feature of tropical shores from east to west, and they even extend into sub-tropical waters. They favour relatively calm seas, and ideal sites for their growth are river estuaries and the backwaters of coastal creeks. On the east coast of Queensland they can be seen in many places marching along the water's edge in dense colonies. Behind their tangled, knotted roots the dedicated explorer can discover a different and fascinating world of plants and animals—but unfortunately mangrove forests are not particularly inviting places to explore because of the hordes of mosquitoes and biting midges that live and breed there.

Although Queensland has its share of inaccessible shores, much of its coastal area can aptly be described as 'tropical paradise'. The scenically beautiful shoreline from Ingham to Cairns, and beyond to Cooktown, has been extensively developed for its tourist potential. The area has everything to attract the visitor: superb climate, forest-clad mountains, brilliant seascapes, golden sandy beaches fringed with palms and casuarina trees. Further north towards Cape York a few tracks lead away from the main coastal route. One of these leads to Weipa, on the western side of the peninsula. Another goes to the peaceful settlements of Portland Roads and the Lockhart River Mission, near which is the magnificent boulder-littered Quintells Beach. Cape York itself is scenically splendid, with its long stretches of sand interspersed with headlands jutting into the vivid waters of the Torres Strait.

CAIRNS, QUEENSLAND
A view of the harbour, from the Esplanade. Cairns, 1863 kilometres from Brisbane, is Queensland's most northerly city.

Top left:
PORT DOUGLAS, QUEENSLAND
Situated beside a magnificent inlet sixty-four kilometres north of Cairns, Port Douglas is a hub for professional fishermen and tourists.

Bottom left:
DARWIN, NORTHERN TERRITORY
Sunsets over the harbour of this tropical city are often spectacular, especially during the Wet season, when the heavy sky glows with colours of fire. With its eventful history and cosmopolitan population, Darwin is a place of immense interest, with a way of life all its own.

Above:
BUCHAN POINT, QUEENSLAND
Between Cairns and Port Douglas there are many superb beaches, some long and straight, others small and curving neatly into the coastline. Many are tucked away between great heaps of rock, or are backed by steeply rising forested slopes. The margins of this lovely beach at Buchan Point, about thirty kilometres north of Cairns, are fringed with palm trees that lend an air of tropical mystery and romance to the scene. Even in winter, Queensland's northern coastal area is blessed with a mild climate, and visitors can enjoy warm sunny days beside the sparkling blue of the Coral Sea.

WYNDHAM, WESTERN AUSTRALIA

This is part of the superb panorama from Five Rivers Lookout on the West Bastion, the rugged range that rears over the town of Wyndham and Cambridge Gulf. Vast expanses of forbidding mudflats blanket the region, their monotony broken in places by fortress-like ranges and the five major streams that empty into the Gulf—the Ord, Durack, Forrest, King, and Pentecost rivers. Near the coast a network of mangrove-lined tidal watercourses patterns the flats. Lying in the far north-western corner of the State, in the Kimberleys, Wyndham is the terminal of the Great Western Highway and a strategic port for northern Australia. It was first established in the 1880s as a supply centre for the Halls Creek goldfields, and later grew into a vital outlet for the pastoral industry. Today the Wyndham Meat Works process and export beef to world markets. As with other northern ports in Australia, a deep-water jetty is necessary to cope with the enormous differences in the depth of tides (Wyndham has a rise and fall of up to eight metres). Tourism is a growing industry in the town, and for nature-lovers there are a number of prolific bird colonies in nearby lagoons.

PORTLAND ROADS, QUEENSLAND

The small settlement of Portland Roads is situated on Weymouth Bay, near the mouth of the Pascoe River on the far north-eastern side of Cape York Peninsula. It was here, in 1848, that the ill-fated Edmund Kennedy left his eight companions while he pushed on to Cape York with the Aboriginal Jackey Jackey. From the goldrush days of the last century until the second World War the port of Portland Roads served miners from the Claudie, Pascoe, and Wenlock rivers; and after this the place became an important strategic base for flying boats. Today there is little evidence of its past history—only a monument to Kennedy and some stumps of the once-magnificent jetty. The dozen or so people who now live here rely mostly on the sea and soil for subsistence. Because of its isolation, there is a wonderful air of serenity at Portland Roads, and most travellers who have braved the rough tracks to visit the little waterfront settlement look enviously at the few simple dwellings with their neat gardens nestling into the surrounding hills. The nearest shop of any kind is at Lockhart River Mission, fifty kilometres away. Nothing, it would seem, could disturb the peace of this place.

Above:
SOMERSET, QUEENSLAND
Mangrove forests are found throughout the tropical regions of the world, and in Australia extensive areas line the northern coast from the far north of New South Wales to Shark Bay in Western Australia. Isolated patches of this rather grotesque vegetation also occur in a few areas of the southern coasts. The most interesting time to see mangroves is at low tide, when the sturdy, stilt-like roots are exposed: however, for those who wish to venture into the forests, it is wise to take plenty of insect repellent! Colonies of mangroves dominate each end of the beach at Somerset.

Top right:
NEAR DERBY, WESTERN AUSTRALIA
North of Derby, the crumpled, rusty-brown Kimberley coastline pushes into the vivid blue waters of the Indian Ocean. Access by sea to this wild and fragmented land is virtually impossible in most places because, as this aerial photograph shows, the shores are well-guarded by treacherous reefs.

Bottom right:
PUNSAND BAY, QUEENSLAND
Punsand Bay, with its lovely wide sweep of beach, lies near the tip of Cape York. Here, bathed in the pale glow of dawn, it seems to contain the essence of tranquillity.

CAPE YORK, QUEENSLAND

Popularly known as 'the tip', the rocky headland of Cape York that protrudes into the brilliantly coloured waters of Torres Strait, is the most northerly point of the Australian continent. (The people on the right of the photograph are standing on the actual tip of the headland itself.) Access to the tip is not easy. Much of the region north of Coen is inhospitably wild, and the only road to the top is that which follows the Bamaga-Thursday Island telephone line. The route is narrow and crosses many unbridged creeks and rivers — and the few that are bridged are not to be tackled by the faint-hearted. The most difficult river to cross is the Jardine, which lies about eighty kilometres from Cape York. Despite its closeness to their goal, many people are not willing to subject their vehicles to the perils of this wide, deep river. But those who do manage to reach Cape York find that the experience is worth all the trials. The views from the higher parts of the headland are magnificent. To the left, a vast expanse of sand sweeps to a distant bluff; to the right, colourful rocky slopes plunge to the aquamarine sea. Lying immediately off the top of Cape York are Eborac and York islands.

DUNK ISLAND, QUEENSLAND

Basking under the tropical sun, in the same latitude as Fiji and Tahiti, Dunk Island lies relatively close to the Australian mainland at Mission Beach, 140 kilometres south of Cairns. Smaller islands, all of them covered with lush tropical rainforest, dot the surrounding waters. Dunk Island is a national park, and well-graded walking paths wind through its superb vegetation from the holiday resort to various beauty points. One of these is the 298-metre high peak of Koo-Tal-Oo, from the summit of which there is a grand panorama of mainland, sea, and islands stretching far to the south. Wildlife is plentiful, and the Brush Turkeys and Scrub Fowl are so used to people walking past that it is possible to watch them busily foraging for food in the undergrowth. Aborigines once lived on Dunk, in the days when it was known as the Isle of Peace and Plenty. The first white settler was Edmund Banfield, author of *The Confessions of a Beachcomber*, who came to this tropical paradise in the late 1800s and lived there until 1923. His grave, which lies near the walking track to Koo-Tal-Oo, bears the inscription: 'If a man does not keep pace with his companions, perhaps it is because he hears a different drummer. Let him step to the music he hears'.

53

Islands

A multitude of islands fringe the Australian shoreline. Most of them are continental in origin: they once belonged to the mainland but became separated from it by submergence or erosion faulting. Some lie in lonely isolation; others cluster in groups, sometimes quite close to shore. They vary in size and character from tiny outcrops of bare rock to towering mountainous masses clothed in dense forest, from shallow mudflats to low cays and atolls fringed with palms.

The largest Australian island is, of course, Tasmania, once linked to the mainland and now a separate entity covering 63 000 square kilometres. A number of remnant-islands lie off its own shores. Melville Island, north of Darwin, is Australia's second largest island, although it is considerably smaller than Tasmania. Its low wooded hills and swampy mangrove flats are populated almost exclusively by Aborigines. Of all the islands off the Northern Territory's coast, Groote Eylandt is probably the best known because of the mining activities.

Apart from some rocky outcrops and Lord Howe Island—a popular holiday spot situated 675 kilometres north-east of Sydney—there are no large islands off the New South Wales coast. Victorian waters are a little better off with French, Snake, and Phillip islands, the latter large enough to support four settlements. Another small Victorian island is the wild and desolate Lady Julia Percy Island, which lies off Port Fairy and is an important reserve for many bird species and a seal colony. South Australia has Kangaroo Island, which has some really spectacular coastal scenery; and just west of where the Bight begins is the start of the Archipelago of the Recherche, an extensive system comprising over a hundred rugged granite islands and rocks that stretch for many kilometres to Esperance Bay. More archipelagoes skirt the Kimberley coast in the far north-west of Western Australia. This State's holiday island is Rottnest, which lies off Perth and is home for the rare and endearing Quokka wallaby.

In number, and for sheer loveliness, the islands off the coast of Queensland top the list. Most of them lie in calm seas towards the north, well protected from heavy ocean swells by the Great Barrier Reef. Many are national parks, and several, such as Hayman, Brampton, and Dunk Islands, have been developed into holiday resorts. There are a few that are impressive in size—like Hinchinbrook, with its peaks towering over 1000 metres—but many are nothing more than forested hills, their shores ringed by rocks and sandy beaches. Others, like Green and Heron islands, are coral atolls. These atolls may lack the grand scenery of the continental islands, but around their shores are some of the best displays of coral and marine life to be found anywhere along the Great Barrier Reef. The latter, one of the great wonders of the world, stretches from Lady Elliott Island, just off the Tropic of Capricorn, and ends near the shores of Papua New Guinea. At the very tip of Queensland, lying between Cape York and the New Guinea coast, and well protected by reefs, rips, and tides, are the Torres Strait Islands, once part of the land bridge that linked Papua New Guinea to Australia.

Of all Australia's islands, perhaps the most interesting is Fraser, which lies in Queensland waters off Maryborough. It was originally formed from sand which over millions of years was borne on ocean currents from the coast of New South Wales, and gradually moulded by winds and tides into what is now the largest sand island in the world. With its wide variety of scenic attractions, it has one of the most intricate and fragile ecosystems to be found anywhere around the Australian coastline.

COCKATOO ISLAND, WESTERN AUSTRALIA
This craggy island lies off the Western Australian coast north of Derby, in the Kimberley region. It is extensively mined for its rich deposits of iron ore.

Previous pages:

KANGAROO ISLAND, SOUTH AUSTRALIA

The Admiral Arch, a wonderful natural arch in the cliffs, is part of the spectacular south-west coastline of Flinders Chase, a national park at the western end of Kangaroo Island. From the car park, situated well above the arch, a rocky path marked by dabs of paint winds down the cliff side towards this extraordinary phenomenon. Its tortuous course seems never-ending; and the sudden appearance of the arch at the end of the descent is the more remarkable. Visitors cannot help but be impressed at its immense size and the spaciousness of the cave below. Kangaroo Island, lying off York and Fleurieu peninsulas, is Australia's third largest island.

Above:

THURSDAY ISLAND, QUEENSLAND

Thursday Island—known to many people simply as 'T.I.'—lies in the Torres Strait about forty kilometres off Cape York, and is the commercial and administrative centre for a large area. It is a small island, with a length of less than three kilometres and a width of only about a kilometre, and has among its neighbours Tuesday, Wednesday, and Friday islands, all named by Captain Cook in 1770. The airstrip for Thursday Island is on nearby Horn Island. Another twenty-one islands, most of them reserves for the Islanders, are inhabited. This photograph was taken from Green Hill, looking towards Prince of Wales Island across the narrow channel that separates it from Thursday Island.

ROTTNEST ISLAND, WESTERN AUSTRALIA

Situated nineteen kilometres off the coast from Fremantle, and easily accessible by ferry or plane, Rottnest has become one of the most popular holiday spots in the west. Much of the island's charm lies in its coastline, which is indented with a multitude of attractive bays and inlets, many of them sheltered by extensive reefs. These reefs are easily visible in the clear water, and their intricate lacy patterns help to give to the island its special fascination and character. To swim in these rocky pools is a delightful experience, and one that has been described as being like swimming in champagne. Rottnest has had an eventful history, as it was a penal colony for many years, from 1839. Some of the oldest buildings in Western Australia still stand there today, painted, as they were last century, in the colour known as 'Rottnest Yellow'. One of the most famous buildings, the Quad, once part of the penal settlement, has now been incorporated into The Lodge, a pleasant guest house redolent with the history of the island. This photograph was taken at Fish Hook Bay, at the far western end of Rottnest. The entire island is now an A class reserve.

Top left:
WHITSUNDAY PASSAGE, QUEENSLAND
Acclaimed as one of the world's loveliest waterways, the Whitsunday Passage extends for more than thirty kilometres, with a width in some places of less than three kilometres. Access is from Airlie Beach, near Proserpine.

Bottom left:
MARIA ISLAND, TASMANIA
This beautiful and historic island lies off Tasmania's eastern coast, between Orford and Triabunna.

Above:
PHILLIP ISLAND, VICTORIA
Phillip Island lies across the entrance to Western Port, 140 kilometres from Melbourne, and is linked to the mainland by a bridge at San Remo. There are four settlements on the island, the main one being at Cowes, a popular holiday resort. Near Cowes there are koala reserves, and elsewhere on the island seals and muttonbirds are found; but one of the best-known tourist attractions is the nightly 'penguin parade', when hundreds of Fairy Penguins come up the beach from the sea to their burrows in the dunes. Shown here are the Nobbies, part of the island's southern coast which is composed of rocky headlands interspersed with excellent surf beaches.

BRAMPTON ISLAND, QUEENSLAND

One of Australia's most popular holiday islands, Brampton lies in the Cumberland Group, thirty-two kilometresfrom Mackay. Nestling among coconut palms and superb tropical gardens on the north-eastern shore of the island, the buildings of the Brampton Island Resort blend well with the natural scenery. The resort is a long-established one, with an enviable reputation for providing an atmosphere of fun and relaxation. It is easily accessible from the mainland, for as well as a deep-water jetty, Brampton has an airstrip, made mostly from reclaimed land. From the air, the island promises much beauty. Headlands of differing proportions, some well-grassed, others clad in a variety of trees including the stately Hoop Pine, jut into the brilliant turquoise waters. Most of the rocky bays and sandy beaches are fringed with coral reefs. With its seven square kilometres of national park, the island begs to be explored. Numerous well-worn walking-paths lead to bays and beaches, and a path also winds up the slopes to the highest peak, which has several magnificent lookouts. The main circuit track is only six kilometres long, and, except for a section that winds through woodland, provides wonderful vistas all the way.

FRASER ISLAND, QUEENSLAND

Fraser Island, a sand island covering an area of 184 000 hectares and lying approximately 160 kilometres north of Brisbane, is one of Australia's most fascinating places. This unique world of sand supports an astonishing variety of natural features. Patches of lush rainforest punctuate heavily timbered woodland; light scrub gives way to heaths, swamps, and perched dune lakes. Everywhere there is sand: on the forest floors, around the swamps, and in vast expanses of naked dunes called sandblows that blanket coastal areas and fall away to wide beaches. On the island's east coast sections of the Seventy-Five Mile Beach are bordered by hills of coloured sands fashioned by the elements into fantastic spires and minarets. Appropriately, these exquisite formations are called the Cathedrals. Only four-wheel-drive vehicles are suitable for travelling around the island, and access is via vehicular ferry from the mainland. For travellers without suitable transport, the best way to see the island is to fly to the holiday resort at Orchid Beach. Situated in a magnificent position on the north-eastern shore, this comfortable hotel provides a number of day trips that cover the most interesting features of the island's kaleidoscopic terrain.